COLOR

IN YOUR HOME

COLOR
IN YOUR HOME

Tessa Evelegh

Special photography by Polly Wreford

NORTH LIGHT BOOKS

Cincinnati, Ohio

COLOUR IN YOUR HOME

First published in North America in 1999 by
North Light Books
an imprint of F&W Publications, Inc.
1507 Dana Avenue
Cincinnati, OH 45207
1-800/289-0963.

1 3 5 7 9 8 6 4 2

Library of Congress Cataloguing-in-Publication Data:
A catalog record for this book is available.

ISBN 0-89134–966–9

A BERRY BOOK
Conceived, edited and designed by Susan Berry for
Collins & Brown Ltd

Editor Amanda Lebentz
Art director Debbie Mole
Designer Claudine Meissner

Reproduction by Hong Kong Graphic and Printing Ltd
Printed by Midas Printing, Hong Kong

contents

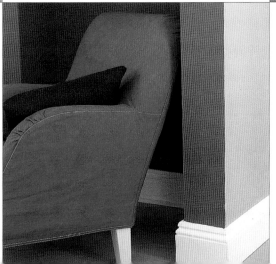

COLOUR AND SETTING

COLOUR IS *a powerful tool in home-making. It creates mood, ambience and above all, impact. The secret of making it work for you is to think of colour in terms of tone. So whether you like neutrals, pastels, mid-tones, brights or deep tones, it is easy to produce the look you want.*

COLOUR SPEAKS volumes about our homes, influencing not just how they look, but how they feel too. Of all the elements in a room, it is the colours that evoke an emotional response, creating an atmosphere of relaxation or cosiness, airiness or excitement. To be able to create such ambience quickly and easily by wielding a paintbrush would be thrilling if it came easily, but for many people putting colours together can often be fraught with anxiety. Faced with a choice of more than 1,500

Right the neutrals

Ranging from white to black through to creams, coffee, taupe and gunmetal, neutrals are always elegant and easy to live with. This dining room with white chairs and navy panels demonstrates the range, offering plenty of contrast for a lively scheme.

Left the pastels

Light, classic colours that will always be favourites, pastels are soothing and cheerful. They can range from white with just a hint of hue to the much stronger tones of the true artist's pastels. Here, sky blue and cream are combined to create a sophisticated room.

colours offered by many paint manufacturers, choosing can be daunting. The main problem is the huge leap of imagination from gauging colour on a tiny swatch to visualizing the effect in the finished room. The human eye can differentiate between literally thousands of shades, yet paradoxically, it's all too easy to 'just miss' – and the colour that looked so glorious on the swatch looks less than impressive when painted all over the walls.

Decorating is a time-consuming business and mistakes are expensive, so the natural response for many people is to play it safe with something undoubtedly tasteful but possibly unadventurous.

This is a real shame because there are simple ways to achieve the look and mood you are after even if you don't have any training in colour theory. The key is to develop an instinct for the shades that work best for you and your home.

Instead of getting bogged down in the received colour wisdom such as 'blue is a chilly colour', which has the effect of writing off all blues and limiting your choice, it can be much more effective to look at the effects of different types of colours. Start by thinking about the type of person you are and the kind of personality you would like to give your home. Do you love the restrained elegance of

Left the mid-tones

Softer than pastels, lighter than deep tones and more muted than brights, mid-tones make a statement yet they create a relaxing mood. The mustard and coriander tones in this room make for a modern yet restrained scheme.

Below the brights

Lively and invigorating, bright interiors create an extrovert look, inspired by sunny climates. This azure and tangerine dining room has a warm, tropical feel.

Right the deep tones

Warm and moody, deep tones create a womb-like ambience. Traditionally favoured by royalty, they are still associated with richness and luxury. They are perfect for bedrooms, as demonstrated by this crushed berry combination.

neutrals or are you a soft pastel sort of person? Maybe you prefer mid-tones that make more of a statement? Do you like brights that spell individuality? Or do you have the confidence to make a statement with exotic deep tones? Each creates a different ambience and can be a valuable key to achieving the mood you're after, yet none restrict you to thinking in terms of whether you like blue, pink or yellow.

You'll find that once you start thinking of colour in terms of tone and type, you'll have complete palettes of colours offering a choice of shades that work happily together. So, for example, put several

brights together, and you'll be surprised what mixes well. However, introduce just one bright to a pastel scheme and it will tend to dominate, whatever colours you choose. Each chapter in the main part of this book looks at a different depth of tone, and within each, there are several   palettes. Let the rooms provide inspiration for more than 100 finished effects and help you to decide on the looks you would enjoy living with.

Armed with the inspiration, you can begin to develop an instinct for the colours that are right for you. The early chapters help you to do this by unravelling some of the jargon and demonstrating

the effects that colours have on one another using 'video' sequences. The book goes on to divulge step-by-step the way professional interior designers develop colour schemes, and demonstrates this by showing you how to create three very different looks from one basic colour.

Given confidence, inspiration and enthusiasm, you can begin to make colour work for you and have some fun playing around with it, which is generally when the most exciting schemes are born. So go ahead and experiment with some new ideas – after all, colour is so much richer than just red, yellow and blue ...

understanding
colour

10

THE BASICS OF COLOUR

MOST OF US *respond to colour emotionally, leaving theory to the experts. But by under-*

standing the vocabulary of colour, and how paint swatches are arranged, you can quickly

learn how to analyze the tones and make them work for you.

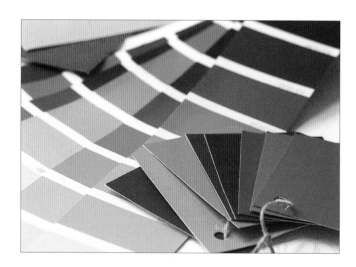

THE PARADOX of colour is that it is both an art and a science. Most of us consider colour theory an art, but as soon as we think we'd like a few clues about how to use colour, we face a jargon-filled science that's fraught with rules. Yet some of the very best schemes break the rules for glorious combinations. Children, unburdened by science and rules, can come up with the most delicious combinations.

CHOOSING COLOURS

Most people know what they like when they see it, but how do you go about putting together an interesting colour scheme, starting from scratch, in your own home? The easiest combinations to put together are monochrome schemes because you use just one hue – blue, green or yellow, for example – and create interest by using several shades of that one colour or adding patterns or textures in the same colour. The classic combination of blue and white is a very successful example of a monochrome scheme. But colour schemes become a lot more exciting and personal when you start to mix the hues. The

Left Colour swatches

Cards and swatches are often arranged so that tones of the same colour appear together and colours within each section appear in the order of the spectrum. Create colour harmonies by using colours near to each other, or contrasts by teaming those that are far apart.

main body of this book arranges colours into tonal types because once you think in terms of tone rather than hue, it is much easier to mix the colours. However, to use tones effectively, you need to be able to assess them accurately. This is easy when you are looking at different tones of the same colour but not so simple when you are evaluating the tones of several different colours. One guideline is to look at the contrast of the colour against white, which acts as a highlight. Another useful skill for colour scheming is to develop an understanding of what a colour is made up of. For example, a green may be more yellow-green, or more blue-green. The best way to do this is to look at lots of different shades of the same colour together.

Paint charts are an invaluable tool for honing your colour sense. Many paint colour mixing units in Do-it-Yourself stores can mix 1,500 colours or more, and there is a colour swatch for each one. The cards and swatches are often arranged in a helpful way – perhaps six tones of the same colour on one card, ranging from light tones at the top of the card to deep at the bottom, and usually in a fan in the order of the colours of the spectrum (see right). Take several paint cards home so you can assess the colour in your own time, away from the distracting artificial lights of the store. Tap into a professional designer's skills by starting with the furnishing fabric, then match up the rest of the colours to the fabric, then follow the plan through step-by-step as described on page 24, and you'll be guaranteed success!

Colour terms

Harmonies

Colour harmonies are the hues that are close to each other in the spectrum. For example, reds, oranges and yellows harmonize with one another, as do greens, turquoises and blues. Tonal harmonies (see Tone) are schemes that use several colours (which may or may not be close to each other in the spectrum) that are of a similar tone and would look alike in a black and white photograph.

Hue

Another word for colour: the identity of the colour. For example, the colour may be blue – any blue from the palest pastel blue to midnight – as long as it is discernable as blue, it will be a blue hue. Black and white do not have any hue.

Primary colours

Pure red, pure blue and pure yellow from which all other colours are mixed.

Saturation

Pure, intense colours. Well-saturated colours are clear and brilliant.

Secondary colours

Colours that are made up of two of the primary colours. Blue and red make violet: red and yellow make orange: yellow and blue make green. Violet, orange and green are the three secondary colours.

Shade

A colour that has black added. These are usually seen as muted, muddy or knocked back.

Spectrum

All the colours of the rainbow which include (clockwise), red, orange, yellow, green, blue, indigo, violet.

Tertiary colours

Colours that are made up of a primary colour and the secondary colour next to it. So, for example turquoise is made up of blue (primary) and green (secondary).

Tint

A colour that has had white added. These are usually seen as milky, chalky or pastel.

Tone

The darkness or lightness of a colour, if seen in a black and white photograph, colours with the same tone would all appear in the same shade of grey.

Warm colours

Hot colours such as reds and yellows appear to 'advance', making a space seem cosy.

Accent

Colour used in small amounts, often in contrast to the main colour. Accents are used to emphasize the main colour scheme.

Colour 'wheel'

The colours of the rainbow arranged in a wheel, commonly used when studying colour theory. In practice, many paint swatches are arranged in the same order and this helps when planning harmonies and complementary schemes.

Complementary colours

Colours that contrast with each other, such as red and green or yellow and violet. They are opposite each other in the colour wheel.

Contrast

Either contrasting colours (see Complementary Colours, above) or contrasting tones, for example a dark colour with a light colour.

Cool colours

Colour theory states that colours at the blue and green end of the spectrum are cool. They appear to recede and lend a feeling of space to interiors. However, lavender blues with pink undertones, for example, are not necessarily chilly so don't be put off a colour because it is theoretically cold.

HARMONIZING TONES

USING HARMONIZING tones creates a much more unified look than tonal contrasts, and can be used very successfully to create unusual colour combinations, provided the colours have a similar tonal value, as this 'video sequence' demonstrates.

HARMONIZING tones are particularly easy to live with as no one colour stands out from the rest, creating a well-balanced look. You can combine a wide range of colours provided they belong to the same tonal range – pastel, mid-tone, bright or deep. Within each range, you can use subtle shifts in tone (deeper or lighter) to create visual interest while keeping an overall harmonious feel.

2 Adding a second colour (left and below)
A second cushion, this time in warm lilac, marries the pale pink cushion to the tones of the chair and wall, creating greater harmony.

1 The first colour (above)
The chair and wall are relatively close in tone while the pale pink cushion added to the chair adds a lighter tone to the picture.

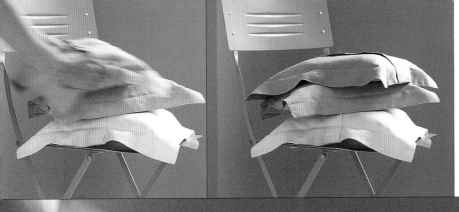

3 Adding a third colour (left and far left)
A further lavender cushion is added to the pile of cushions, and links the cushions more closely to the chair and wall colours.

4 Adding a fourth colour (above and left)
A fourth cushion in turqoise blue, of a slightly paler tone, shifts the balance of tones back towards the paler end of the spectrum. These four colours work together because of their close tonal values.

CONTRASTING TONES

The most obvious contrast of tone is black and white but colours

that are deep or light in tone can be put together to create schemes with a

dramatic intensity.

Tonal contrasts do not have to be monochrome, as here, they can also be colourful but they rely on deep colour contrasted with a much lighter colour. Like a photographic negative, the contrasts can be pale on dark, or dark on pale.

1 Adding light to dark (below)

A grey sofa with a matching deep toned cushion contrasts with a pale wall behind. A second cushion in pale tones emphasizes the contrast and links the sofa to the wall.

2 Adding a second light tone (bottom)

A further pale cushion creates a greater area of contrasting tone and a more balanced effect between wall and sofa.

3 Adding a third colour (left and below)

Adding a third colour, in a mid-tone, helps to bring harmony to the scheme by bridging the tonal gap between the pale and dark tones, creating a 'friendlier', less dramatic look.

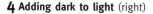

4 Adding dark to light (right)

The same sequence is applied in reverse to a pale sofa, this time set against a pale background, adding first a single dark cushion, then a couple more to increase the proportions of the contrasting tones, and finally a mid-tone to bring the area together. Compare the overall effect of tone – the mass of dark tones on this page looks cosy and comfortable, the mass of light tones on the right hand page looks airy and elegant.

MIXING COLOURS

MIXED COLOUR SCHEMES are the most adventurous and often create

the most exciting effects. Yet they are extremely simple to put together if you

keep the colours close in tone, as illustrated by this 'video sequence'.

MANY PEOPLE find mixed colour schemes more difficult to put together than single ones – especially since it is all too easy to be tripped up by conventional colour wisdom, such as keeping to hot colours or cool colours. This scheme makes use of hot pink and cool turquoise and it works because the contrast is not overly strong, so no one shade 'jumps out'.

2 Adding a second colour (left and below)
A flash of fuchsia provides a colour contrast to the turquoise, while teaming with the lilac wall. The cushions are close in tone, so that the fuchsia does not dominate.

1 The basic scheme (above)
A turquoise chair looks striking in a lilac room. The closely matching cushion gives a solidity to the furniture.

3 **Adding a third colour** (above and right)
*The purple cushion adds an extra
dimension, creating a truly mixed scheme.
However, all the tones are very close,
which ensures a cohesive look*

4 **Adding accessories** (far right)
*Introducing purple accessories, such as the
lampshade, balances the whole scheme.*

COLOUR PROPORTIONS

THE QUANTITY *of any given colour will affect the overall look and you can play with these quantities to change the way that a scheme looks, while using the same mixture of colour.*

IN THIS example, a coloured tablecloth with green and blue checks provides the background. Using differently coloured china on the cloth demonstrates how one colour or another becomes the dominant player in a colour scheme. You can try this out at home with swatches of fabric and wallpaper.

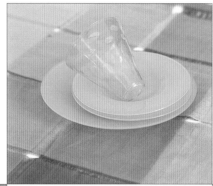

1 Left
Lime-coloured china placed on the cloth emphasizes the sharp green tones of the background cloth, picking up these colours and adding a citrus zest to the scheme for a lively, modern look.

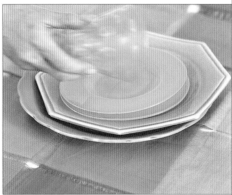

2 Left and right
Blue and turquoise plates added to the lime green china bring out the blue tones in the cloth and take away from the sharper, more limey colours in the cloth.

3 Right
Remove the lime green china and the proportions change again, this time creating a distinctly softer, more blue-toned feel to the whole display, with just a hint of citrus used as an accent.

COLOUR ACCENTS

INDIVIDUAL SPOTS of colour, usually in a strong contrast to the main shade,

can be used to bring a colour scheme to life, and can also be used to focus attention

on a particular object or colour.

WHILE HARMONIZING colour schemes are very easy on the eye and particularly relaxing to live with, they can look monotonous without the injection of the odd spot of colour as a contrast. This contrast has the effect of accentuating the quality of the main colours. Remember that less is more in decorating, so use these accent colours judiciously. The more the accent contrasts with the main colour, the less of it should be included in the scheme.

1 Far left

A harmonizing tonal scheme composed of lemon and lime mugs on a lime cloth makes a harmonious but uneventful-looking composition.

2 Above right and right

Adding a contrasting tone in the form of the kingfisher blue of the inside of the mug changes the focus of the composition. The flash of contrasting colour (roughly one sixth of the area) brings the colour scheme to life without dominating it.

planning
for colour
22

PLANNING A SCHEME

IT'S NOT DIFFICULT *to give your home personality with interesting*

colour schemes – simply follow the professional steps on these pages and

take inspiration from the three very different lime schemes that follow.

THE EASIEST way to give your home a new look is to change the colour scheme, yet putting one together can be daunting. Mistakes are expensive and time consuming … and can hardly be hidden in the back of the cupboard like a fashion disaster. Many of us are tempted to play it safe, which is why paint manufacturers have responded for so many years with a plethora of whites that have just a hint of colour. While these are invaluable, we also crave interiors with more individuality.

So what if you want something bolder? Where do you start? The most reassuring piece of advice is not to do anything in a hurry. Professional interior designers don't just pluck a colour scheme out of thin air; they take their time and research it and make up storyboards. Here's how to do it.

1 Look for inspiration (right)

There's inspiration for colour schemes all around. Just take a walk down the street and look at trees, plants, flowers, shells on the beach, moss on a wall, two cars parked next to each other. Get a feel for the kind of colour combinations you like. In nature they can be extraordinary and unexpected like the rich green of moss with rust-coloured autumn leaves; the purple veins running through the green of an ornamental cabbage leaf; the orangey reds and greens on apples. Carry an instant camera with you wherever you go, so you can capture delicious colour combinations to store in a scrapbook. A few inspirations have been collected at the beginning of each chapter to get you going. You can also find inspiration in magazines. But don't just flip through. Tear out pictures of any colour combinations you like. The other place you might find a source of inspiration is in your own home. You might have some favourite accessories, such as a piece of china, furnishing fabric, napkins or a bedspread, for example, that inspires an interesting colour scheme.

2 Collect swatches and accessories (top right)

Go on a trip to your favourite shops. Find several swatches for each requirement: furniture, curtains, cushions, walls. Collect as many small swatches as you want – these are usually free at this stage. You may also want to buy a piece of china, a single napkin, anything that you really love that sets you off on a colour scheme. Collect paint chips from the paint shop and carpet or flooring swatches, too. Don't feel a need to make decisions at this stage – simply ponder on your favourites once you get home.

3 Make up a storyboard (right)

Choose your favourite fabrics and colours, and stick them into the book in about the same proportion as they will be seen in the room. So, for example, if you're going to have cushions in an accent colour, cut a very small piece of this swatch to stick down, and a larger piece of the fabric for the curtains. Paint in brushtrokes of paint. Some for walls, some for woodwork, some for furniture.

4 Try it out (left)

Swatches are all very well but they're fiddly to look at. They also encourage mistakes. To really assess the finished effect, you need to look at the colours from the same distance you would see them in the room. So, there's no use holding a piece of flooring close to, as you would a book – throw it on the floor and stand on it. Look from there. Fabrics need to be draped on chairs or hung at windows. So the next thing you need to do is to order larger swatches or short lengths of everything. Buy a 50cm (about $^1/_2$ yd) length of fabric to hang at the window and a small pot of paint. Paint the colour onto lengths of wallpaper lining and hang it on different walls in the room as the light will react very differently on each wall. Hang the fabric, drape it over furniture, manoeuvre a chair into position until you have a mini section of the room 'done'. That way, you can have a really good idea of what it's going to look like. Live with it for a bit. Look at it at different times of the day, or even at different times of the year if you like. Once you really know you're happy, you will have the confidence to go ahead and order.

Bright style

THREE LOOKS *for the same lime-coloured room show how to create*

your own style using colour. Here, for a bright, young interior, lime is

teamed with blue. Turn the pages for two very different moods.

1 The inspiration (left)

Usually put with citrus shades, such as lemon or tangerine, lime can look just as good with other brights, such as clear cornflower blue. The intense blue of the napkins set against lime-green plates provided the inspiration for this scheme.

2 The accessories (left)

A favourite cornflower-blue salad bowl and a little blue-checked vase of miniature chrysanthemums make great accessories in a lime and blue room.

3 The storyboard (below)

With lime green and cornflower blue in mind, the hunt was on for a linking fabric for the curtains. Blue and green checks were the perfect answer for a lively young look. A green and white check tablecloth would link the colour of the walls with the pattern of the curtains.

4 Try it out (left)

A length of fabric is pinned up at the window against the lime-green wall. The vase of cornflowers, stood on a lime-green runner, represents other blue elements in the room.

Bright, young style

Lime green and azure blue make a vibrant combination, reminiscent of the bright green leaves of spring set against a cloudless azure sky. The checked curtains contain both colours, linking the green walls with blue furniture. They also incorporate several other limey tones plus sharp yellow, all of which add depth to the whole scheme. The choice of checks keeps the style of the room young and fresh to complement the lively colour scheme. The overall look is modern, but this room demonstrates how to achieve a new look, even if old furniture, such as the side table, needs to be incorporated. In this case, a simple lime-green runner updates it, in keeping with the rest of the room.

Elegant appeal

LIME IS *not regarded as a 'safe' colour, but neither does it have to be acid-edged. Team it with white and pale wood, choose clean, modern lines to furnish the room and you have an elegant interior.*

1 The inspiration (left)
Sharp lime-green chrysanthemums look stunning against pure white.

2 The accessories (below)
Simple white plates and a lime-green napkin demonstrate a modern simplicity that's easy to live with.

3 **The storyboard** (left)

An uncomplicated storyboard becomes more sophisticated when you bring in texture. The paint and napkins are the only representation of lime. A heavy white damask cloth and crisp white translucent organdie provide contrast in colour and texture.

4 **Try it out** (below)

A simple square dish of green pears set against the lime wall lend a feeling of both the colour and style of the room.

Pure elegance

Simple, restrained and elegant, the combination of lime and white is pure and uncomplicated. Translucent white organdie curtains reflect light back into the room, giving it an airy feel, and this is complemented by a white tablecloth, white china and accessories. The pale wood furniture is tonally compatible with the rest of the colour scheme, carrying through the feeling of light. The choice of monochrome grey and white paintings continues the peaceful mood, which could have been destroyed by a jarring contrast. The clean, uncluttered lines of the chairs, china and accessories set an elegant style which benefits from being kept sparse.

Classic yet contemporary

LIME IS *often seen as bright and contemporary, with no place in a pretty, traditional scheme. Here, it looks glorious with the deep pink tones of English roses and foxgloves.*

1 The inspiration (above)
A bunch of roses, fresh from the garden, look delicious next to the high key tones of lime green.

2 The accessories (right)
A pile of favourite rose-decorated French plates, a pretty trellis and rosebud fabric and two tones of green napkins inspire the ambience.

3 The storyboard (left)

Wonderful English country-style printed fabric links the pinks and greens of the walls and accessories and co-ordinates with the pink and green trellis fabric for the tablecloth.

4 Try it out (below)

A jug of palest green hydrangeas on the blue table next to the curtain swatch looks stunning next to the lime-green wall.

Fresh and floral

The pinks and greens of an English country garden make a classic and evocative combination. Here, the deep pinks of the printed fabric appear to deepen the lime-coloured walls, giving the room a fresh and pretty look that is a lot less predictable than a traditional pastel treatment. The trellis tablecloth and rose-printed china pick up on the curtain design to carry through the country garden theme. The blue side table works here because it is tonally similar to the flowers on the fabric. Extra blocks of fresh colour have been introduced by the napkins in two tones of green to give the whole room a timeless, classic look with a fresh modern slant.

the
neutrals

38

NEUTRALS

inspiration

T<small>HE</small> <small>EXQUISITE</small> <small>BLEACHED</small> *tones of
weathered wood, old stone, smooth
pebbles on the beach and chunky
rope provide endless inspiration for
easy-to-live-with neutral schemes.*

W<small>HETHER</small> <small>YOU</small> <small>LIVE</small> in the country,
by the sea or in the city, a walk outside is a
treasure trove of inspiration for neutral
schemes. There are soft, grey tones of
weathered wood on the forest floor, cliffs,
sand, pebbles, driftwood and old rope by
the sea; stone walls and buildings in the
city. Perhaps it is the abundance of neutrals
around that give us a relaxed sense of well-
being when in neutral rooms.

The outdoors doesn't simply give us the
'broad-brush'. Look closely and you'll find
variations of tones and accent colours that
can be the beginnings of very sophisticated
combinations. The tones of tree bark offer
light and shade; lichen on an ancient brick
wall demonstrates how breathtaking subtle
grey-green can look against stone tones.

NEUTRALS

influences

NEUTRAL IN *tone and easy to live with, stone,*

straw and wood are among our most ancient

building materials. Their natural, solid appeal

has formed the backbone of traditional

decoration throughout the centuries.

AFTER THE decline of the Roman Empire and up until the Italian Renaissance, stone, straw and wood provided the main palette of early decoration in western Europe. In intervening eras, this simple form of decoration has sometimes been regarded as unimaginative – yet interiors decorated with natural materials always have integrity and an air of peace. When interior fashions have veered away from elaborate ornamentation (which can disguise less-than-beautiful proportions) they have tended to move toward elegant forms of architecture and furniture, which are generally enhanced by neutral colours. This is what happened in early 18th-century Europe when Biedermeier furniture, with its boxy but curvy shapes and cherry or walnut veneers, became popular. Nearly 100 years later in Germany, the formation of the Bauhaus School in 1919 led to simplified interiors with fitted furniture that instigated the Modern Movement. A well-known contemporary, French arhitect Le Corbusier, also concentrated on practical, streamlined interiors that demanded the combination of clean white interiors set off by natural woods, chrome and steel.

Top

Shaker simplicity is reflected in unvarnished wood and cream walls.

Above

A classic coffee and cream interior and Empire-style bed show how elegant neutrals can be.

Right

Light-toned woods, like maple, are particularly suited to neutral interiors. Combined with black, they become sophisticated yet pure in both line and colour.

WHITE ON WHITE

Always elegant, white has a calming effect that works both in period and in contemporary homes. Each surface, material and texture shows a slightly different tone of white, which is one of its advantages. Variations add to the overall depth of the scheme and you really don't have to be too meticulous about matching.

Pure and fresh, white makes a statement and yet is undemanding. It is easy to get right because it will never clash and, when whites are teamed together, the overall effect is one of calm, their slightly different textures and tones adding interest to the room. Even if the furniture and accessories are quite different in style or even age, white has a unifying effect. Architects and designers love white because it emphasises the three-dimensional quality of space. In any room, surfaces are brightened and shaded by the light, which enhances the shapes and highlights architectural detail. White works best when you use pure natural fabrics such as linen or cotton because if they get marked (which they inevitably will), you can simply soak them in a weak solution of bleach to give them a new lease of life. So if you love the white look, choose loose covers for the furniture and simple unlined curtains and dispel the myth that white can't be family-friendly.

Right

The lack of colour in white schemes means that texture takes on a more important role than in rooms of stronger hues. Here, texture is added with looped coir flooring and painted panelled walls. The panels are accentuated by shadow, adding interest to the scheme.

Left

*Texture plays a
leading role in
white schemes.
Here, translucent
blinds and heavily
slubbed upholstery
provide visual
contrast.*

Below

*Crisp white
bedlinen has
universal appeal
and always looks
fresh when teamed
with white voile,
muslin or bleached
linen curtains
and drapes.*

Right

*When brought together
with white, the
voluptuous curves of
the washstand and bath
are perfectly happy
cheek-by jowl with
the simple modern
curtains and
chequerboarded floor.*

4 5

RICH CREAM

CREAMY SHADES HAVE a softness and warmth that endows them with feminine appeal. Just like white, cream works well in both period and modern homes, but because it is mellower you can afford to use it in a more sumptuous way, choosing flamboyant drapes and voluptuous, curvy furniture.

CREAM ON CREAM will always lend an air of sophistication. Creams can be mixed with confidence and, like tones of white, a mismatch will, if anything, add depth to a scheme. But you need to be a little more careful with creams than with whites. They work better if you keep either to the more yellow buttery creams, or to the more blue-green creams. Whichever you prefer, cream loves texture which is all the more highlighted in the absence of colour. Contrast smooth linens and shimmering mother-of-pearl buttons with thick, scrunchy knits and heavily slubbed silks. Dress creams up with a touch of gold, or give them a timeless honesty by teaming them with natural materials like coir, natural wood and jute.

Right

Natural, unstained wood and cream make a relaxing blonde-on-blonde scheme for a modern dining area. The clean lines of the wood cupboards and trestle table legs provide a strong architectural structure that sets off the comfortable curviness of the paler upholstered chairs. Cream on cream patterned curtains add interest without being obtrusive.

Right

This cream and caramel bedroom offers a rich but relaxing haven, concentrating the eye on the inviting forms of the four-poster bed and the sofa at its foot. The cream fabric on the sofa, the heavy weave of the bedhangings and the roughness of coir carpet all focus the attention on texture and form.

COFFEE AND CREAM

COFFEE AND CREAM *has a cool sophistication that doesn't cloy. Ranging from pale cappuccino to sultry espresso, you can use accessories to mix the proportions to taste. Coffees look wonderful teamed with the grey bloom of limed wood, or with natural timber and coir matting.*

ALWAYS ELEGANT, ever tasteful, here is a combination that is easy to get right because it looks strongest when just one tone of coffee is teamed with cream. Leaning towards knocked-back greys rather than the reddish earthy tones, coffee colours are easy to live with and make an excellent choice for living rooms. Neither overtly masculine nor intrinsically feminine, they can be coaxed into either direction. Use pale *café au lait* for a soft feminine look or darker coffee colours for a bolder, more masculine look. Alternatively, use small accents of dark espresso for definition in a mainly cream scheme. Historically, coffee and cream spells confidence, coming into fashion during forward-looking times of optimism, such as in the post-war 1950s.

Right

Soft café-au-lait tones and scrunchy texture give this bedroom a rich, voluptuous feminine look. Cooler than cream, the palest coffee lends an air of sophistication and elegance.

Above

Coffee has a soft grey tone that is perfectly complemented by the gentle bloom of limed wood. Here, coffee upholstery looks wonderful against the limed wood of the chair frame and side table. The pale cushion on the chair links the two.

Right

*Simple coffee
check curtains
give a clean,
modern accent to
a country-style
cream interior.*

Above

*The mix of simple
geometrics and
more cream than
coffee gives this
room a classic
feel. The scheme is
given depth by
using the same
tone of coffee
in different
proportions
with white.*

MIXED TAUPES

Neutrals veer towards cool greys in one direction and warm browns in the other. Taupe is where they meet. Simple neutral schemes choose tones of the same colour, but there's nothing to say you can't mix them, and the result is usually an easy-to-live-with interior that exudes confidence and sophistication.

WHEN WARM beiges and cool grey tones are mixed, they exude confidence yet, because they are never harsh, they can never jar. But be warned: when you mix the taupes, you need to be bold. This is a statement that needs to be made with confidence, otherwise it could look like a mistake. As the light levels go down, the eye finds it increasingly difficult to differentiate between greys and beiges, but the larger the area of colour, the easier the eye can cope. Paint blocks of it on the walls if you dare; or keep the walls plain and choose furniture and fabrics in neutrals from both the grey and brown taupes. The easiest way to get the colours right is to search out fabric that combines the tones, then match up the rest of the interior.

Right

Mixed taupes look best when at least three are combined to give the scheme a cohesive look. Here, the furniture is in warm brown tones while the main blocks of colour on the walls are cool grey. The warmer strip of paint between the main block and the chair provides a mid-way point that links the two.

Left

Let professional designers mix the taupes for you. Search out some furnishing fabric that combines the tones, then match the rest of the scheme to those. Here again, the fabric shows the use of three tones against cream. Splashes of colour from both the grey and beige end of the spectrum are given definition by the charcoal ammonite.

Right

Mixed taupes also work well in traditional interiors. Here, the blue-grey wall makes a mid-way link between the beige cupboard and grey chair. The neutral quality of all the colours lend emphasis to the elegant, curvy forms of the French-style furniture.

NEUTRALS AND BLACK

NEUTRALS AND *black make the strongest colour contrast of all, the ultimate being black and white. This polarisation usually makes for smart, stylish schemes that tend to be associated with contemporary city interiors. However, the versatility of neutral and black colour schemes ensures that they will look just as at home in a traditional country cottage.*

THE SUCCESS of strong contrasts lies in the proportion of each colour. A little black simply adds definition to a mainly cream or white scheme . The more black you add, the progressively bolder the results. Generally, black and white interiors are more elegant than pretty and more suited to geometric or abstract patterns than traditional florals. However, softness can be introduced using accent colours.

These are particularly important with black and white schemes, relieving the starkness while lending importance to the contrast. Choose strong bright colours, such as the primaries, bright turquoise or fuchsia, to set off black and white. As you only need very small amounts of accent colour, you can change them regularly to give the room a fresh seasonal look.

Right

A mainly cream scheme is smartened up and given definition with a boldly striped chair and black giraffe-skin style cushion, transforming a potentially safe interior into something much more exciting.

Right

This black-and-white chequerboard hearth and smartly striped chair seat lend smart city chic to a mainly white room

the
pastels
54

PASTELS
inspiration

Everyday household items, such as bars of soap and woollen blankets in delicate pastel tones, summer flowers, foliage and even fruit bring endless inspiration for adventurous schemes.

Exquisite soft tones can show up on everyday household items, offering inspiration in the most surprising places. A bundle of children's chalks, stacks of soap and even a prosaic pile of dusters can trigger ideas for fresh new interior schemes.

Play around with the colours, taking one away, perhaps, or adding another, until you have a combination that pleases. The world of nature can often offer even more surprising combinations. Young artichoke heads in palest green may be blushed with a hint of pink; a green striped melon, when cut open, could reveal soft apricot flesh. Summer flowers, too, and palest green spring leaves can be a source for endless inspiration.

PASTELS

influences

Used in ancient times to create beautiful frescoes, pastels became highly fashionable in smart French salons during the reign of King Louis XV, when the rococo style was born.

Pastels were much in favour with Madame de Pompadour, mistress of King Louis XV of France. Her taste for pretty shell and powder pinks, blues, turquoise, lilacs and apple green set the style for smart French salons in the mid-18th century. The colours complemented the delicate, feminine furniture, heavily ornamented with scrolls, shells, ribbons and flowers. This was the style known as rococo, enthusiastically copied from Spain to Russia and up into Scandinavia. These pretty pastels really suited the soft northern sunlight, creating airy interiors which were adopted with enthusiasm by the Swedes, who softened the tones with grey. For maximum light reflection, they painted both furniture and walls in muted turquoise, pinks, blues and greens, teamed with white. Pastel colours were used in ancient times, too, notably in frescoes, the elaborate wall-paintings of the classical Roman period. These colours were incorporated into neoclassicism, an architectural style that became popular in the late 18th century. Inspired by the discoveries of original Roman buildings in Pompei, it was developed in Britain by Scottish architect Robert Adam.

Top
Robert Adam decorated using motifs such as classical vases and loved to mix pastels.

Above
Pastel yellow and lilac combine on the outside of this house in the south of France.

Right
Pastel blues with white and gilt lighten this Swedish neoclassical interior, a style that followed rococo at the end of the 18th century.

PASTEL AND WHITE

PRETTY PASTEL schemes are freshened by white for perennially popular combinations. Choose a monochrome combination such as classic blue and white for an uncomplicated scheme that is easy to live with, or layer on more pastels. The trick is to team pastels of the same tone for a unified look.

ESSENTIALLY FEMININE, pastels and white are a charming choice for bedrooms and bathrooms. Keep the room pretty with sprigged patterns or choose checks for a cleaner look. For bolder, more contemporary interiors, use solid blocks of pastels set against white. Whatever the style, if you are using several pastels, they will look best if they have the same tonal value. The contrast between pastels and white is relatively subtle, which makes the combination easy on the eye and relaxing to be in. If some or all are patterned, the best way to achieve this is to look at them from the distance you would see them in the room – because that can change your perception of the overall colour. While large areas of pastel against white are very easy to see at distance, fine detail in pastel against large expanses of white may hardly register. This is because the eye will tend to 'mix' fine all-over patterns and see a single tone scheme. However, the light the room receives may influence your decision.

Right

Pastel blue and white check is a classic winner. The stripes on the folded fabric are actually navy blue and red but they are very fine and set against a large proportion of white, so the eye reads them as a similar tone to that of the chair.

Right

*Sprigged florals
and tiny checks
look charming
together in pink,
green and white.*

Above

*Bold zigzagged
stripes in pastel
blue teamed
with pink and
white check
make a clean
combination.*

61

FONDANTS

The chalkiness of fondants transforms baby colours into something much more sensuous that both harks back to the classic rococo style and looks forward to simple modern living. Fondants look best in crowds. A team of several in the same tone creates impact because they set each other off, while too much of one colour is in danger of becoming lost, as the eye becomes immune to its hue.

SOME PALETTES look best with the same colour layered tone on tone. Fondants aren't like that. They look best in packs because by using several hues in the same tone, it is their delicious chalkiness you end up emphasizing. There's nothing remotely masculine about the fondants, but used wisely, they need not be sickly. These are tones that are soft but strong. Two fondants together can verge on the sickly, but a third sharpens up the scheme and brings wit and style to the whole interior. You can use them with cream for a cooler, more subtle combination, or on their own for a richer scheme. Irresistible in tactile soft velvets, fondant pastels are equally as gorgeous in fresh modern crisp linens and cottons.

Right

Timber mouldings painted in mixed fondant pastels and arranged randomly on narrow shelves make a pretty three dimensional display, bringing colourful interest to a traditional interior. It works because the pastels are of a similar tone to the rest of the room.

Right

Pretty chalky pink and blue teamed with plenty of white to freshen them up, makes for an unfussy, yet ultimately feminine interior.

Left

Soft velvets in fondant shades just beg to be touched and are a perfect fabric choice for this feminine palette. The smooth curvy lines of the chairs and chequerboard table combine for a deliciously sumptuous modern interior.

Below

Here, the more predictable lilac and pink fondant shades have been given extra zest with lime.

PISTACHIO TONES

THE DELICATE yellowy-greens of the inside of pistachio nut kernels provide surprising inspiration for elegant interiors. Their subtle tones make for unexpected yet sophisticated, harmonized schemes that look wonderful teamed with pale natural materials such as wood, rush and willow. Add depth to the scheme by combining lighter and deeper tones of pistachio.

LIGHT BUT NOT too bright, pale but not sugary, pistachio is easy to live with without being safe. A pistachio room implies individuality, yet this is a stunning colour scheme that is easy to create. The key is to harmonize the colours. Choose a base shade, then add depth by introducing lighter or darker tones of that same colour. The overall look will be one of soft elegance. Don't automatically paint skirtings and architraves (baseboards and trimwork) white just because that's the traditional way of doing things. Without white, the look will be softer and more elegant: with white, it will look smarter and more regimented. Use tiny checks and sprigged floral fabrics for a pretty look; bold geometrics for a more modern feel. Think natural for accessories – the gentle tones of pistachio look wonderful complemented by pale wood, rush and coir.

Right

The use of matt and gloss finishes gives definition to different tones of the same colour. Inspired by the cushion fabric, this wall was first painted in a chequerboard of two different tones of matt paint, then shiny chequers were rolled over the top.

Right

Pistachio chequers again, but with a homespun-style checked cloth to give it a country look. Three tones of paint add depth, but retain the harmony by avoiding white for a light and airy springtime feel.

WATER COLOURS

THE SOFT, WATERY shades that linger around pale turquoise have a subtlety of hue where the borderline between aqua blues and greens are blurred. This makes them a joy to use because they can be teamed with so many colours, ranging from limey greens through the turquoises and watery blues to lilacs.

THE AQUA hues are a pleasure to live with because they have a light and airy feel yet offer definite colour, even in the lightest of tones. The clearer shades look great as a colourwash, which emphasizes their wateriness. If you choose the slightly greyer shades, they begin to look more period, very like the Gustavian colours of 18th-century Sweden. Despite classic colour wisdom that blue and green should never be seen together, blue and green turquoises can be very happy together, especially when they have the same tonal value. These colours are easy to put together because they flow naturally from one to another. Turquoise becomes more blue, lavender and lilac in one direction, more green and lime in another. You can keep to just one or two shades, mix several, or use an accent from one end of the range to sharpen up colours that are mainly from the other end.

Right

The softer, greyer versions of aqua give an elegant and romantic period feel, especially favoured in traditional Swedish interiors. The pink-lilac throw offers a sympathetic accent to the green aquas of the rest of the scheme.

Right

In this restful scheme, blue-aquas set off the mainly green-aqua theme, with lilacs and lavenders that progress on from the blue end of the palette providing accents for emphasis.

Left

A green-turquoise wash on this simple clapboard summerhouse has been set off by watery blue striped upholstery. White paint keeps the interior light, while stencilled motifs in the same paint as the exterior link inside and out.

Below

Softest aqua shades are an ideal choice for the bathroom, complementing the watery nature of the room.

SUMMER SKIES

CLEAR YELLOW AND cool blue is a happy combination, evoking the yellow sun in a blue sky. This is nature's inspiration, which makes it universally appealing and rooms decorated in these colours will always be welcoming. The key to success is to choose clear shades for vibrant schemes.

LIGHT AND BRIGHT, yet warm and welcoming, the colours of summer skies are always pleasing because these are the hues that remind us of the best of times. They lend the room a relaxed, inviting ambiance, often creating the happiest environments. Even cold, north-facing rooms take on a relaxed summery feel when treated to this colour combination. This classic blue and yellow combination was a favourite of the the French Impressionist Monet, whose yellow dining room opened into a blue kitchen. The sky colours look brilliant together on their own. Choose lighter and deeper tones if you'd like to add extra depth to the scheme. Then, if you want a sharper look, add accents of tangerine, nasturtium orange and lime green. For a softer, more feminine feel, add touches of soft rose pink.

Right

Elegant yet unaffected, this smart yellow and blue sitting room demonstrates decorating with confidence. The accents of green and rust offer an element of surprise while lending depth to the whole ensemble.

Right

A simple blue and yellow scheme makes for a relaxing bathroom. The unpainted wooden shutters and twiggy planters lend a country feel while the limey green of the plants helps to sharpen up the scheme.

ARTIST'S PASTELS

FUN, CONFIDENT AND *lively, the artist's pastels are the strongest pastels of all, threatening to encroach on the brights. These schemes are assured. Use them on their own or mix them tutti frutti style – although you should keep to the same tone if you don't want some to recede and others to dominate.*

FLAMBOYANT AND young at heart, these are the true shades of the artist's materials that lent their name to pastels. Although strictly speaking, these colours are quite strong tonally, they contain a lot of white which gives them a chalkiness that is often associated with pastels. Artist's pastels can be used singly for impact, or in teams of two, three or more different colours against a main background. They also work well with white as it provides a crisp foil for their chalky tones. Avoid teaming them with clear, saturated colours as these will have the effect of making the pastels look milky and cloying. Artist's pastels are a brilliant choice for rooms where you want a positive colour that will never become overbearing.

Right

A stone-coloured fireplace and chair covers are an ideal foil for artist's pastel green walls. The accents in a slightly darker tone of chalky mauve emphasize the green.

Opposite

Warm apricot walls provide the perfect backdrop for a tutti frutti of artist's pastel chair covers.

he

tones

72

MID-TONES
inspiration

All the natural vegetable dyes belong to this palette, so it's easy to find good matches in nature itself. Take inspiration from the flora and fauna around you for some surprising combinations.

Late summer and early autumn lends endless inspiration for mid-tones. Think summer berries, plums, apples and pears ripening on the trees. Notice how green summer leaves gradually become edged with reds and yellows as autumn approaches; how they fall onto mossy green forest floors.

You can rely heavily on nature for mid-tones inspiration as these are the shades produced by natural vegetable dyes, so they are easy colours to match. Record unusual combinations with an instant camera, and don't be daunted by trying them out at home. These gentle muted tones can sit happily next to the most unlikely partners.

MID-TONES

influences

MID-TONES, *often muted with grey, can be the most relaxing of all to live with. This is because they are probably the closest shades to traditional colours made with natural pigments that were extracted from the local environment – from the earth and plants.*

THE TERRACOTTA tones and spicy shades of earth colours, such as ochre and raw sienna, are traditional shades for buildings. Used in intricate patterns to decorate African huts, they can look wonderfully elegant in a Palladian villa. But mid-tones are more than just earth colours. Think of knocked-back olive greens, ox-blood red, warm pink and blue-green Wedgwood, all shades that can be extracted from plant dyes. This is the palette of 18th-century Europe and American Shaker communities. In Europe, wood-panelled walls, doors and skirting (base) boards were often painted the same colour throughout for a cohesive look, in contrast to the recent tendency to pick out woodwork in white. The Shakers generally painted walls in white, picking out skirting and pegrails in a colour. This soft muted palette was one that also attracted William Morris, the renowned late 19th-century English designer, who reacted against the new synthetic dyes by using only natural dyes to produce his designs of flora and fauna in shades of greens, blues, peaches, reds and browns. By the turn of the 19th century, these blue-greens were brightening a little into the purer turquoises, typical of art nouveau.

Above

The art nouveau influence on style and colour filtered down to the meeting places of ordinary men and women. This eel and pie shop in London dates back to 1910.

Right

Turn-of-the-century art nouveau introduced brighter colours to the traditional palette, though they were still by no means strong. Peacock blues and greens were a typical combination, used here in London's Harrod's food hall.

Left

Soft pinky terracotta plaster, marble details and a deeper-toned chequerboard flagstone floor combine to create a classical mid-toned interior.

CHINA BLUES

INSPIRED BY TRADITIONAL Chinese porcelain, clear blue teamed with crisp white has been a decorating favourite for centuries, yet it still has fresh appeal. Keep it clean and simple, or add other tones into a basically blue and white scheme for a more elaborate look. Blue and white geometrics always look smart, while florals and patterns lend a more feminine feel.

So SIMPLE YET so beguiling, clear blue and white never fails to please. Down the centuries, it has been picked up and turned into a classic by many different cultures. During the 18th century, the blue and white traditional Chinese pottery inspired the English potter, Josiah Spode to produce the still popular willow pattern china and also the Dutch potters in the town of Delft, which is still known for its blue and white tiles.

Yet the same combination can still look clean and modern in contemporary interiors. Perhaps that is because it retains a lightness and prettiness without being overtly feminine or fussy. The greatest joy of blue and white is that it will always succeed, and even those who believe they have no colour sense whatsoever can be confident of good results. The more adventurous can add in tonal accents for a more sophisticated look.

Right

Classic blue and white can be an excellent starting point for a more complex scheme. Here, it has been given extra depth with the introduction of toning greens and lavenders. It is the predominance of clean blue and white that keeps the overall look fresh and simple.

Right

French toile de jouy is seen here with traditional blue and white Willow Pattern china. By keeping to a monochrome colour scheme such as this, you can mix several patterns, yet still retain a cohesive look.

LAVENDER HUES

LAVENDER, WITH *its undertones of pink that bring it close*

to purple, is the warmest of blues, and the best choice for colder

north-facing rooms. It can be teamed with complementary

pinks for prettier, more feminine rooms, with greys for an elegant

modern look, or with deeper blues for added richness and

a wonderful feeling of luxury.

MANY PEOPLE shy away from decorating with blue because they see it as a cold colour. Lavender blues are not like that. Tinged with pink, they have a natural warmth that can be boosted with toning rose or heather shades. Lavenders are undemanding and easy to live with, yet have a subtlety that gives them an air of sophistication. Lavender pigment does not exist in nature, so this did not become a popular colour in interiors until the last century when synthetic pigments were developed. So lavender usually has a contemporary look and the most successful interiors acknowledge this, rather than work against it. The easiest way to achieve this is to team lavender with white, which gives it a sharp edge.

Right

The purple hues of lavender and violet have been used in tones that range from large areas of almost pastel to the very deep accents. Again, white has been used to lend crispness.

Left

Lavender cupboard doors provide the basis for a strong but elegant scheme. The pinker heathery tones on the chair and throw add depth, while the broad grey stripe on the throw cools down the overall look.

Right

Deeper lavender hues are accented with a pinker tonal heather shade for a scheme with depth. The whole look has been cleaned up with white.

SUMMER BERRIES

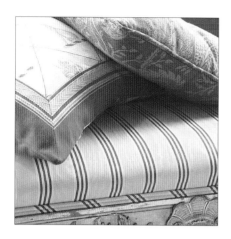

STRAWBERRY AND RASPBERRY colours evoke the glorious freshness of summer fruits. They combine the strength of red with the softness of pink, and so are neither harsh nor overly feminine. Keep them smart by choosing geometric checks and stripes, or teaming berry shades with cream for glorious interiors that evoke summer all year long.

FRESH SUMMER FRUIT colours teamed with cream were a favourite combination of traditional Swedish style. Take inspiration from their timeless interiors by combining these colours with strong geometric patterns if you want to avoid an overtly feminine scheme. The strawberry tints that veer more towards the orange end of the spectrum will create the freshest schemes; for a more feminine look, choose the more purply pinks of raspberries. Although it is usually safer to keep to one or other of these, they can be teamed if you throw in enough different shades. One strawberry and one raspberry shade could look like a mistake; three or more different ones are likely to be far more successful. Soft greys and celadon greens make particularly good companions for berry schemes.

Right

The more purple shades of crushed raspberry have been given emphasis by a bold checked bedcover. Green accents on the bed end sharpen up the scheme.

Right

These cushions show how well raspberry and strawberry shades can work together. The large-checked cushion at the bottom of the pile and the pom-pom trimmed cushion incorporate both shades.

Above

This traditional Swedish colour combination of strawberries and cream has timeless appeal that still looks fresh today. The paler strawberry stripes on the chair add depth to the colour scheme.

MUTED MIX

ELEGANT AND *sophisticated, muted colours can be easily mixed without fear of clashing. These are mid-tones that have been softened with a touch of grey, making them less demanding than the stronger tones and very easy to live with. Tested over time, muted colours have long been traditional favourites both in Europe and North America.*

THE SOFT, MUTED shades – sage greens, mellow blues and plaster pinks – that were so familiar in traditional 18th century homes are still hard to beat. Although we are no longer limited by the natural pigments that dictated these schemes, they are still alluring, offering a gentle bloom that cannot be recreated in synthetic colours. With the sharpness of tone taken out, the colours can sit more happily together. When they're muted, terracotta and turquoise, gold and green harmonize happily with traditional neutrals. To create this soft, antique look, keep the tones within a limited range so that no one colour predominates. It is a useful device when you have different furniture styles and ornaments, as it automatically unifies the scheme.

Right

Terracotta, turquoise and natural wood are lifted by upholstery and flooring in golden tones – a heady mix indeed, but given classic muted tones, they add up to a relaxing interior.

Left

*Muted shades mix
well with naturals.
Here, the stripped
wooden shutters
and heavy neutral
curtains are lifted
by turquoise and
gold upholstery.
The end result is
both restful
and gracious.*

Right

*Muted mid-tones
take on greater
importance when
set against a
pale neutral
background, as
shown here,
where the drapes
become a feature.
The plush covered
chair continues
the colour
through, while
the grey-blue
washed furniture
brings tonal
harmony to the
whole room.*

TERRACOTTA TONES

The TAN TONES of terracotta are a perennial favourite, much-loved by artists for setting off their paintings. Strong and warm without being overbearing, terracotta is a classic that comes from natural pigments, so it will never be a passing trend. Traditional or contemporary rooms look terrific in terracotta. Try teaming it with neutrals for a cool, sophisticated look and gold and yellow for a sunny feel.

THE WARMTH of terracotta looks wonderful in north-facing interiors where the light is bright but cold – immediately lending cosiness and intimacy to the room. Earth tones are the colours of our natural environment, offering comfort and a sense of security. For centuries, when only natural pigments were available, paints were often tinted with earth tones, lending an individual personality to each neighbourhood. This can still be seen around the countryside in the interiors of old inns that have not been modernised and re-decorated. Terracotta looks just as good today, and its reassuring tones can give rein to highly adventurous schemes. Terracottas look wonderful with neutrals, and can be used on one wall, or in blocks to give depth to neutral rooms.

Right

Team terracotta with cream for a light, modern and elegant look. Here, the cream bathroom leads off pleasingly from the terracotta landing. Carrying complementary colours through to adjacent areas like this gives the whole house a cohesive feel.

Right

This colour scheme was inspired by the glorious terracotta and gold brocade throw on the sofa. A stunning golden yellow wall plaque breaks up the intensity of the terracotta walls for a rich but unpretentious interior.

MIXED SPICE

THE FLAVOUR of spices may be hot but their colours are surprisingly subtle. Think muted mustard; the yellowy earth colours of cumin and coriander and black peppercorns and you'll have the beginnings of a mixed spice scheme. If you want to heat it up a little, add accents of red hot chilli, but don't overdo it, or, just as in a recipe, it will tend to dominate.

IF YOU LOVE THE warmth of earthy colours but find many of them just a touch too dark and overbearing, spice shades should fit the bill. Far more subtle and sophisticated than many earthy shades, the spice colours occupy the yellow end of browns and look fantastic teamed with black for emphasis. Here is a palette that can be elegant and restrained when used as plain blocks of colour, or decidedly wilder if you add tonally

compatible animal prints. Yet even if it's used in this less conventional way, the subtlety of the colours mean you won't quickly tire of the room. Spice shades take on a richer look when teamed with dark wood furniture. Add creams and neutrals for a cleaner, more modern look. For accent colours, take inspiration from other spices – red hot chillis to warm it up, or subtle pale green cardamom colours for a cooler effect.

Right

Animal prints look fabulous with classic spice shades such as cumin, coriander and black pepper in an interior that is less than tame, yet is unlikely to date.

Opposite

Cream cools the spice shades for an elegant look. Touches of hot chilli red in the carpet emphasize the cooler aspects of the scheme

BRIGHTS
inspiration

For this modern palette, you may take inspiration from modern materials like plastics, aluminiums and laminates as well as the most vibrant of flowers and foliage.

LIVELY AND invigorating, nature inspires bright combinations all year round. Think of yellow and blue spring flowers set off by vibrant green, summer fields of poppies and sunflowers and winter holly berries, nestling in glossy green leaves.

Even the everyday can offer interesting combinations, such as shiny new cars in the streets, children's toys, jars of candy and plastic picnicware. Bright colours abound in modern materials like plastics, aluminium and powder-coated metals. Or search out Chinese or Indian supermarkets where even the packaging can be vibrant. You can find packets of tea, rice and noodles with labels in startling combinations such as pink, turquoise and red.

BRIGHTS

influences

IN THE BRIGHT light of hot climates, you can afford to be brave with vibrant colours. Close to the equator, even nature dresses in exotic tones. The flowers are brighter than the delicately toned natives of more temperate climes and birds of paradise display feathers in glorious, brightly coloured combinations.

TAKE INSPIRATION from the brightly painted houses of Mexico, the Caribbean and the Mediterranean. Europeans traditionally chose more muted colours that suited the soft light of their climate until the end of the 18th century. In the latter half of that century Scottish architect Robert Adam, and his younger brother James, inspired by the architecture of ancient Rome and Greece, brought in brighter colours such as blues and greens. The whole of Europe was influenced by this classical revival, manifesting iteslf as the Empire style during the Napoleonic era in France, which embraced bright yellows and greens. These pigments were often expensive to produce, so only the wealthy could afford these fresh new colours. However, once synthetic aniline dyes were developed, there followed an enthusiasm for bright colour. Yellows, turquoises, purples, reds and bright blues were more readily available, and this was reflected in the brighter tones that began to appear in some of the more adventurous homes at the turn of the 20th century.

Top and right
Bright colours are popular in hot equatorial climates where the strong sun complements their vibrant tones. In the Caribbean, they break all the 'rules', using clashing colours to great effect – as demonstrated by these beach huts and shopfront on the island of Mustique.

Opposite
Inspired by Mexican style, this washroom bravely combines emerald, blue, turquoise, purple and cinnamon to great effect.

TROPICAL HUES

Vibrant tropical colours are always uplifting. They're bright and lively, yet have more subtlety than the basic primaries. Tropicals love to band together, offsetting each other. One contrasted against the background of another makes for a rich interior: several set against white will sing out.

Tropical hues make for extrovert interiors. Take inspiration from the vibrant tones of equatorial climates: turquoise and blue sea colours set against the clear fruity tones of limes, mango, papaya and banana and the strong colours of local blooms like the pinks and purples of bougainvillea. They can be used in twos or threes, or even piled one on another against a rich background for a powerful impact. Or use them in blocks against white for a clean, modern-looking scheme. Alternatively, you can use tropical colours as accents, introducing small amounts of just one into a more muted scheme to lend impact to the other colours. However you use this joyous, clear-toned palette, do not be shy with it. These are flamboyant colours that look most effective when used boldly.

Right

Lime and fuchsia pink cushions lend impact to a turquoise sofa. The vase of mango-toned gerbera flowers adds sharp accent, teaming with the lime cushions to balance the pink and turquoise. Set in a white room, the ensemble is very vibrant.

Right

The unexpected combination of glowing turquoise and rich lavender makes for a glorious interior. The colours are well saturated but because of their clarity they are not overbearing.

CHALKY BRIGHTS

WHITE ADDED to brights endows them with a chalkiness

for a look that is stronger than pastels, more subtle

than primaries. They really can be mixed and matched with

abandon – provided that you choose colours

which retain the same amount of chalkiness to achieve

a balanced overall look.

MATT CHALKY BRIGHTS are reminiscent of traditional Mediterranean paints and, despite their lack of translucency, lend a sunny feel to rooms. Chalky blues, turquoises, yellow and greens formed the popular palette of the 1950s in reaction to the post-war gloom. At that time, it was fashionable to use blocks of colour, even on the outside of buildings. This can still be effective inside, though pattern and texture add interest. The safest way to use chalky colours is to mix and match hues that share the same amount of chalkiness. However, they can also be used as a background for more translucent tropical brights, lending depth to the overall scheme.

Right

Chalky blue and white offer an opaque background for a collection of more translucent, tropical, bright vases, thereby highlighting and making a feature of them.

Right

Broad stripes of chalky lilac and lavender wallpapered onto a white wall make a refreshing and easy-to-live-with interior. The chalky green chair provides a compatible accent colour.

SOFT LIMES

THE GLORIOUS, CLEAR tones of lime are surprisingly easy to live with.

Lime is not as sharp as the other citrus hues, and is probably

mis-named. The colour we call lime is actually more akin to the bright

green, new spring leaves than the mossy tones of the fruit.

It teams happily with all the other clear spring colours – yellow,

pink, blue and purple.

LIME IS ONE OF the easiest greens to live with as it contains a high proportion of yellows, which reflects the light and lends a sunny ambience. Deeper greens are inclined to absorb the light and can have a deadening effect. Lime makes an excellent choice for a garden room, as its spring leaf tones go well with the natural greens in the garden all year round. They lift the darker greens of full-blown summer, harmonize with bluey greens and brighten the dead of winter. It is probably this compatibility with nature that makes light limey greens so easy to live with. There are few colours that they don't team well with. Choose classic citrus shades for sharp modern schemes; muted ballroom blue for a cooler, sophisticated look, sapphire blues for a young feel and rose pinks for more traditional homes.

Right

Jauntily teamed with a blue, red and yellow quilt cover, lime takes on a young, light-hearted look.

Right

Limes don't have to demand citrus partners. Here, the generous amounts of cream plus muted ballroom blue accents make for an elegant and timeless interior.

CITRUS ZEST

BRIGHT, BRASH and invigorating, citrus colours lend a sunny feel to any room. Lemon, tangerine and lime make up the basic palette. Choose one for a pure colour scheme or mix two, or even three, for guaranteed vibrancy. Keep to the hot hues for impact, or cool it down with touches of white.

CITRUS BRIGHTS LEND fresh, clean appeal to the room. This is partly because the colours are pure and well saturated, not 'muddled' with the addition of black, or given a chalky feel with white. It is also because we associate citrus with freshness, which is why many household cleaners are scented with lemon. These are schemes that will always look young and zingy, bringing warmth and light to the room. A mix of tangerine and lemon is particularly sunny, the orange shades emanating heat and the yellow adding a mellower light. When refreshing citrus greens are added to these hot, bold colours they cool down the overall scheme, yet because all the colours are strong they work brilliantly together. If you want a slightly calmer effect, intersperse bold citrus hues with white.

Right

Tangerine accessories lend warmth and impact to a sunny dining area with lemon walls. The natural wood table and chairs and coir flooring add a soft natural feel.

Left

A tangerine chair and fireplace teamed with strong lemon walls make for a happy, sunny room. The lemon and tangerine have similar tonal values, which perversely makes the whole interior more restful.

Right

White walls and the white background to the sheets provides strong contrast to the more intense chequered bedlinen, throw and upholstery. The white both cools down the colour and emphasizes it within the room.

PRIMARY MIX

THE PUREST colours of all, primaries are sometimes seen as unsophisticated because they are favoured in children's drawings. But used well, primary schemes can look clean, modern and confident. Choose one primary to team with white or use all three in a lively combination. Checks, stripes or geometric prints work well for bright, modern interiors.

RED, YELLOW and blue are the colours from which all others are mixed – given help from black for shades and white for tints. So by definition, they are pure and can make powerful statements. Primaries are bold and look best in blocks of colour. Make a scheme around just one, team two or even use all three. Add blocks of black to intensify the colour or splashes of white to sharpen it up and make it more contemporary. Primaries work well with both. They can be happy with emerald greens, too, but add any other colours and you could run into trouble. The problem will be that other colours will be inclined to recede – looking too muddy if they're muted, too chalky if they're tints, dead if they're too deep, too insipid if they're pastel. So for impact, stick to primaries.

Right

The unfussy lines of an elegant modern sofa upholstered in primary red demonstrates a confidence in style and taste.

Opposite

Red, yellow and blue can look fabulous together and if you're clever with pattern, the scheme need not be simplistic.

CLASHING COLOURS

BRIGHT LIGHT HAS the effect of softening the intensity of colour, which is why stronger hues are often used in brilliant combinations in countries nearest to the equator. Follow their lead and don't be shy with brights. They often look better and have much more impact when they're all thrown in together for an extrovert and invigorating scheme.

BE BRAZEN with brights – they can look fabulous when combined without compunction. If they clash a little, so much the better. If you like the look, but lack confidence, take inspiration from hot countries like the Caribbean and Mexico where colour reigns supreme. The extrovert medley of hues they come up with make for thrilling combinations that would never have been seen if their authors had worried about 'getting the colours right'. You can always use their hot clashing combinations as inspiration and tone them down a little if you feel they may not sit so well in colder climes. The trick is to keep them to the same tone as each other, so where the colours may seem incompatible, the tones provide continuity.

Right

Azure, emerald, fuchsia, reds and oranges work brilliantly together here – such a combination would look equally good in a cool climate.

Left

*Terracotta and pink
are an unlikely
pairing, but they work
well together in sunny
climates where the
brilliance of the light
balances the
clash of colour.*

Right

*Turmeric yellow,
emerald green and
sapphire blue make a
lively mixture
reminiscent of sunshine,
trees and sky.*

HOT AND COLD

SOME OF *the best colour schemes break all the traditional rules. Conventional colour wisdom says that combinations should be either hot or cold, yet all of these interiors cross the hot and cold boundary. Yellows, pinks and oranges are hot; blues, greens and purples are cool. Here, they are linked confidently with strong, bright tones.*

SURPRISING SCHEMES that buck the received wisdom are often the most successful. They depend either on outstanding talent or on a happy accident, and when they work, it's with panache. There is nothing wrong with discovering a stunning colour scheme by accident – throwing out the rulebook can result in inventive combinations, which is why children, uninhibited by 'taste' can come up with glorious combinations in their paintings. But some of the more adventurous colour schemes may ultimately prove difficult to live with, so take

your time and try it out before going ahead. Paint a corner of the room and hang up a length of fabric at the window or over the arm of a chair, then live with them for a few days, or even weeks, to get a good idea of the effect. Once you're happy, you can decorate with confidence. It will be well worth it, since the adventurous schemes that do succeed are always the most satisfying because of their originality. These appealing hot and cold colour schemes refer to little else that has gone before them, which makes them all the more accomplished.

Right

Deep purple set against bright yellowy lime, its complementary colour, provides an invigorating contrast of warm and cool colours. Yet on their own, the main colours have a mellow quality. Orange accents lend extra spice.

ight

ot yellows,

range and cool

ellowy limes

ake a zingy

ombination with

ool blues.

Above

A mix of hot

yellow and pink

with cool deep

navy accents

shows colour

confidence.

the
deep tones
110

DEEP TONES
inspiration

*The deepest tones can be found on
greengrocer's stalls, where glossy
skinned fruits and vegetables reflect
the light to show off their rich
and royal hues.*

Look for warm, rich tones at the
greengrocer: cherries and blueberries in
summer; blackberries, red cabbage and
red onions in the autumn. Or research
some combinations in the draper's store,
looking for rich deep pile velvets and
chenilles, perhaps teamed with gold
braids and tassels.

Outdoors, the forest provides glorious
combinations, such as dark green fir
against deep brown branches; fir cones
on the mossy forest floor; copper beech
leaves, etched against a twilight sky.
Inspiration can come from overseas, too.
Search out pieces of Japanese lacquer in
deepest red or black, their glossy surfaces
reflecting the light.

113

DEEP TONES

influences

TRADITIONALLY THE luxury of the wealthy, the pigments of deep, richer hues were often extracted from semi-precious stones and metals, such as the deep blue of lapis lazuli, the green of malachite, copper nitrate and exotic plants, such as indigo, which was imported from India.

INCREASED TRADE between Europe and the East in the 17th and 18th centuries saw an increased interest in rich red textiles for orientally inspired schemes – but these were mainly for the wealthy who could afford them. Another, purer red tone of Chinese and Japanese lacquerware, began to be introduced into Europe in the 18th century, and has gone in and out of style ever since. Terracotta became a popular backdrop for hanging gilt-framed pictures, as it was said to bring out the hues of the paintings, and, being a deep colour, it allowed the paintings to reflect the light. Everyday deeps included drabs and greens. Traditionally, elaborate deep-toned interiors are married with reflective materials such as gold leaf, brass or copper, to bring light to the scheme and add further richness to the interiors. The ultimate deep tone, black, has a much more modern pedigree. Although used in small amounts to enliven schemes, it was not until the 1920s and the introduction of art deco that it became used as a wall colour. To give it a modern look, it was often teamed with silver-coloured metals such as chrome and aluminium, and is still in vogue today.

Below

Black was a popular art deco 'colour'. The huge monometal (early aluminium) murals help to bring light to the glossy black surfaces of the foyer of London's Express building.

Right

Irridescent and metallic mosaics lend sparkle and richness to the elaborate deep-toned interior of Debenham House in London, which was completed in 1907.

Left

Deep tones can be well saturated, as demonstrated by the beautiful peacock blue tiles that decorate Debenham House.

RICH REDS

DEEP RICH REDS, *redolent of Arabian nights, Katmandu and the Indian subcontinent, always lend an exotic air to a room. Perhaps influenced by the colonial age when new decorative ideas were being brought back from the East, these were styles that became popular in smart homes during the 19th century.*

THE RICHEST reds found in rubies and garnets lend a sumptuous, warm and intimate feel to any room. These are colours that are often enriched by artificial light and are at their best in rooms such as dining rooms that come alive in the evening over dinner. The glorious patterns, often incorporating golds and turquoise, give life to this, the most exotic of colour schemes. Pattern is a key factor in this rich look. It can vary from the intense small patterns of traditional paisley to larger patterns of flowers and fruit redolent of Jacobean embroidery. Deep blues,

dark greens and mustard yellows are often combined in these patterns and the lighter gold and mustard tones are useful for adding finishing touches that lighten it. Deep colours are particularly useful for creating warmth and intimacy in large rooms, or those with high ceilings. Red, in particular, is valuable for rooms with a naturally cold light. It is also ideal for bedrooms, creating a feeling of security and comfort. Bed drapes in thick woven damasks, chenilles or velvets enhance this atmosphere, as does dark wooden furniture or deep claret-coloured wallpapers.

Right

Touches of turquoise lend cool relief to ruby reds piled one on the other. Deep pile velvet and shiny silks offer a variation in texture that makes this scheme work.

Above

Gold brings light to a deep red bed throw. The reddish earth brown hues of the walls keep the scheme tonal, allowing the eye to adjust to the richness of the scheme. One tone throughout would look spartan and unwelcoming.

Left

Patterns and textures can be used to lift reds, adding interest to a rich scheme. Strong colours like these usually work best when used in small proportions within an interior that is less intense overall.

AUBERGINES

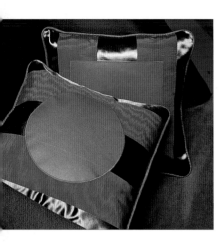

THE DEEP plummy purple shades of aubergine (eggplant) are among the most sympathetic deep tones. They verge on neutrals, hovering between deep taupe and charcoal, but their subtle purple hue gives them added life. You can enliven aubergines further with shimmery fabrics and shiny surfaces such as pewter, silver and gold.

FALLING SOMEWHERE between the elegant restraint of neutrals and the mystery of purples, aubergine makes for unexpected and sophisticated interiors. Since aubergine tones are deep, they lend an intimate and cosy feel, making them perfect for use in rooms designed for entertaining. Whether they veer towards the more blue-purples or those that are rather pinker, aubergines look terrific with metallics such as gold, silver and pewter, since these lend a touch of brilliance to the interior without bringing in too much of a contrast. Shiny fabrics, too, look especially appealing in aubergine. Look for good quality heavyweight velvets and satins that will bring a sense of luxury to the room. Whether you prefer the traditional or the modern look, choose pale or mid-toned furniture in materials such as metal, painted or naturally pale wood. Choose woods such as beech, birch and limed oak, rather than highly polished mahogany or dark woods, which could look a little sombre and overbearing with aubergine.

Right

The truer, pinker tones of aubergine have a modern look, especially when teamed with cream furniture. Fabulous when decorating the whole room, this tone would also look great painted in blocks on just one wall of a mainly cream room.

Right

When teamed with white, this aubergine at the palest and bluest end of the range takes on a pretty and elegant look that is enhanced by the addition of plenty of gold.

DEEP CONTRASTS

DEEP TONES teamed with white make up one of the most starkly contrasting palettes. But far from jarring, the white lifts the deeps and also accentuates the intensity of the colour. This is a particularly good combination for bathrooms as many have white suites, yet deep tones make for very relaxing interiors.

RICH TERRACOTTA, bottle green and deep aquamarine – these are classic comfort colours that lend an intimacy to any room. Yet if the whole room were decorated in just the one shade, it could become overbearing and oppressive and the eye would become immune to the colour, so it would be difficult to appreciate the richness of the tone. These deep colours can all too easily appear to turn black. The best

antidote is, surprisingly, white. It brings a lightness to the scheme and a contrast that accentuates the deep-toned hue. The contrast is strong and the overall effect tends towards the masculine. This colour scheme is best for rooms that are used mainly in the evenings or at night time when it is dark outside, because they provide a womb-like feeling of comfort and security.

Right

The pink undertones of deep terracotta give a warm feeling to this bathroom, which is accentuated by the gilt picture and mirror frames. The whole scheme has been lifted by the white bathroom suite.

Right

Aquamarine, especially when teamed with white, is smart, yet more feminine than the classic deep tones. Blue-green eucalyptus leaves are a perfect tone mid-way between white and aquamarine, softening the whole scheme.

Above

Bottle green and white is a classic combination that is smart and unfussy. A white ceiling and tiles reflect the light, adding brightness to what could otherwise be a dark interior.

NAVY BLUES

SMART AND timeless, navy blues have the capacity to work with almost any style. Traditionally, only the wealthiest homes could be decorated with these inky indigo tones because the pigment was expensive to produce. We don't have that restriction nowadays, and navy can make up some of the smartest modern schemes.

DEEP, YET undemanding, navy blue is a comfort colour, often chosen for uniforms because it always looks smart and suits every colouring. The same goes for interiors. Navy can never be in bad taste. It doesn't clash. It works as a harmony, it works as a contrast. The simple lines of modern upholstery look stunning in navy, as do curvy traditional Chesterfields. Because navy is so deep, it is easiest to live with when used as an element in the room, such as for the furniture, cushions or a rug, rather than as the dominant colour on walls. The deep tone of navy can tend to go very dark and flat, so this is a colour that responds well to texture. The relief of, for example, panelling on walls or heavily textured fabrics for curtains and upholstery adds an extra dimension which catches the light to show off the true beauty of the colour. Teamed with white as a monochrome scheme, navy always looks fresh and smart. For harmonies use close tones of mid-blue, lilac and lavender and for a complementary scheme, use vibrant red.

Right

Navy and white may seem incredibly simple, yet it always looks smart because of the strong contrasts.

When painted on the walls, navy creates a rich, intimate feel. If you love the navy tones, but feel a whole room could be overbearing, use it to paint blocks of colour on a white wall.

Right

The lavender and navy checks on this bed harmonize beautifully with the navy bedhead, while bright red adds a lively complementary accent colour. The result is a fun, yet relaxing bedroom.

BLACK

STRONG, BRAVE *and surprisingly effective, black smacks of independence and confidence. Black has no hue. Tonally, it is as deep as you can go. Black is also uncompromising. It is usually used in small amounts to lend definition to a scheme ... but don't write off using it as a main colour!*

THERE IS only one true black (although there are many near-blacks) and it goes with absolutely everything. Black does not shout but it demands attention. Like anything extreme, black makes a statement. Where you can make it work for you is in the proportions in which you use it. Tiny rooms can look fabulous painted entirely in black, and it can work in larger rooms too. One trick is to use a gloss paint that acts as a mirror and reflects light back into the room. Another way to use black is to team it with a vibrant bright to bring energy to the scheme. Even in small proportions, black will add definition to almost any other scheme. The more you use, the bolder the effect. Black lacquer can add a touch of the exotic to almost any interior, be it traditonal or contemporary. But you should be careful when teaming black with pastels. Black contrasts with pastels so strongly that it can overpower them, so should be used in only the smallest amounts. When teamed with brights, which provide less of a contrast, you can afford to be bolder with your use of black.

Above

A tiny cloakroom looks stunning painted entirely in black save one panel, which is in bright turmeric yellow. The black is painted in gloss, which effectively reflects the light.

Right

Although not the main ingredient of this room, the black and white chequered cloth is the element that makes the statement. Without it, this yellow studio could have felt traditional.

Above

Even larger rooms look great in black. This kitchen is painted in black gloss to improve light levels. Teamed with bright green, the scheme becomes lively, rather than oppressive. Strong colours combine well with black because they brighten the interior without creating too harsh a contrast.

INDEX

ACKNOWLEDGEMENTS

A huge thank you to the team that has made this book possible: to Susan Berry, who has skilfully guided it from conception to production; Polly Wreford for her stunning photographs; Debbie Mole for her elegant design; Sara Bird, for her energy and assistance on photography days; Mandy Lebentz for her sensitive editing and Claudine Meissner for helping with the design. Finally, thanks to the following, who so generously lent their merchandise for photographs: **The Blue Door**, 74 Church Rd, London, SW13 9HH. (plain double bedhead, Gustavian-style painted mirror and bedthrows, pages 38-39, glass outdoor candlesticks, pages 72-73, omelette dish and pans, pages 110-111). **Grand Illusions**, 2-4 Crown Road, St Margarets, Twickenham, Middx TW1 3EE. Mail-order catalogue 0181-744 1046 (painted cupboard, pages 54-55). **Sanderson**, 112-120 Brompton Rd, London SW3 1JJ. (curtain and tablecloth fabric, pages 36-37). **Sofa workshop**, Head office, Boxall House, East Street, Petworth, West Sussex GU28 OAB. For stores telephone 01798 343400. (sofa and covers, pages 16-17).

PICTURE CREDITS:

KEY – R: RIGHT; L: LEFT; C: CENTRE; T: TOP BR: BOTTOM RIGHT; BL: BOTTOM LEFT; TR: TOP RIGHT TL: TOP LEFT: PH: PHOTOGRAPHER

p6: Robert Harding, *Homes & Gardens*, ph. Polly Wreford; p7: *Ideal Home*; p8-9 TL: Robert Harding, *Homes & Ideas*, ph. Dominic Blackmore; BC: The Interior Archive, YMPA; TR: Interior Archive, ph. Cecilia Innes; p42-3 TL: Interior Archive, BL & R: Robert Harding, *Homes & Gardens*; p44-5 All Robert Harding, TL: *Homes & Gardens*, ph. John Mason; BL: ph. Trevor Richards; TR: *Homes & Gardens*, ph. John Freeman; BC: *Homes & Gardens*, ph. John Mason; BR: *Homes & Gardens*, ph. Elizabeth Zeschin; p46-7 TL: Robert Harding, *Ideal Home*, ph. D. Lewis; BL: Helios Collection by John Wilman Fabrics and Wallpapers; R: Robert Harding, *Homes & Gardens*, ph. Jonathan Pilkington; p48-9 All Robert Harding, TL: *Country Homes & Interiors*, ph. Polly Wreford; BL: *Homes & Gardens*, ph. Tom Leighton; TR: *Homes & Gardens*, ph. Polly Wreford; BL *Country Homes & Interiors*, ph. Polly Wreford; BR *Homes & Ideas*, ph. Polly Wreford; p50-1 All Robert Harding,TL: *Country Homes & Interiors*, ph. Polly Wreford; BL: *Homes & Gardens*, ph. John Mason; TR: *Country Homes & Interiors*, ph. Christopher Drake; BR: *Homes & Gardens*, ph. Hugh Johnson; p52-3 TL & BL: Robert Harding, *Ideal Home*, ph. Nadia Mackenzie; R: Robert Harding *Homes & Ideas*, ph. Polly Wreford; p58-9 TL & R: Interior Archive, Schulenburg; BL: Debbie Patterson; p60-1 All Robert Harding, TL: *Homes & Gardens*, ph. Chris Drake; BL: *Homes & Gardens*, ph. Polly Wreford; TR: *Homes & Gardens*, ph. Christopher Drake; BR *Ideal Home*, ph. Tom Leighton; p.62-3 All Robert Harding, TL: *Homes & Gardens*, ph. Tom Leighton; BL: *Country Homes & Interiors*, ph. Jonathan Pilkington; TR: *Homes & Gardens*, ph. Tom Leighton; BL(R) : *Homes & Gardens*, ph. Simon Upton; BR(R): *Homes & Gardens*, ph. Tom Leighton; p64-5 BL: Robert Harding, *Homes & Gardens*, ph. John Mason; R: Robert Harding, *Homes & Gardens*; p66-7 All Robert Harding, TL & BL: *Homes & Gardens*, ph. Chris Craymer; TR: *Homes & Gardens*, ph. Simon Upton; BC: ph. G. Rae; BR: *Homes & Gardens*, ph. Simon Brown; p68-9 All Robert Harding, R: *Homes & Gardens*, ph. Tom Leighton p70-1 All Robert Harding, all *Homes & Gardens*, TL & BL: ph. Tom Leighton; R: ph. Jan Leighton; p76-7 TL & BR: ph. John Freeman; TR: Interior Archive, Schulenburg; p78-9 All Robert Harding, all *Homes & Gardens*, TL: ph. David Montgomery; BL: ph. Jan Baldwin, BR: ph. Polly Wreford; p80-1 All Robert Harding, TL, BL & TR: *Homes & Gardens*, ph. Jan Baldwin; BR: *Ideal Home*, ph. Tim Imrie; p82-3 All Robert Harding, TL: *Homes & Gardens*, ph. Richard Holt; BL: *Homes & Ideas*, ph. James Merbell; TR: *Country Homes & Interiors*, ph. Christopher Drake; BR: *Woman & Home*, ph. Steve Dalton; p84-5 All Robert Harding, TL: *Homes & Gardens*, ph. Hugh Johnson; BL: *Country Homes & Interiors*, ph. Andreas Von Einsiedel; TR: *Country Homes & Interiors*, ph. Andreas Von Einsiedel; BR: *Homes & Gardens*, ph. Jan Baldwin; p86-7 All Robert Harding, TL: *Homes & Gardens*, ph. Trevor Richards; BL: *Woman & Home*, ph. Debi Treloar; R: *Country Homes & Interiors*, ph. Simon Upton; p88-9 All Robert Harding, TL & BL: *Woman & Home*, ph. Debi Treloar; R: *Country Homes & Interiors*, ph. Simon Upton; p94-5 All Interior Archive, TL & ML: Schulenburg; R: Cecilia Innes; p96-7 All Robert Harding, TL: ph. David Parmiter; BL: *Homes & Gardens*, ph. David Parmiter; R: *Homes & Gardens*, ph. Polly Wreford; p98-9 TL: Robert Harding, *Homes & Gardens*, ph. Polly Wreford; BL: Robert Harding, *Homes & Gardens*, ph. Trevor Richards; R: 'Vibe' Collection by Coloroll; p100-1 TL: 'Vibe' Collection by Coloroll; BL: Robert Harding, *Inspirations*, ph. Sandra Lane; R: Robert Harding, *Homes & Gardens*, ph. Jan Baldwin; p102-3 All Robert Harding, TL & BR: *Inspirations*, ph. Spike Powell; BL: ph. James Merrell; TR: *Homes & Gardens*, ph. James Merrell; p104-5 All Robert Harding, TL: *Inspirations*, ph. Debbie Patterson; BL: *Ideal Home*, ph. Polly Wreford; TR: *Homes & Gardens*, ph. Polly Wreford; BR: *Homes & Gardens*, ph. James Merrell; p106-7 All Interior Archive, TL &TR: ph. YPMA; BL & BR: ph. Cecilia Innes; p108-9 All Robert Harding, TL: *Homes & Gardens*, ph. Tom Leighton; BL: *Homes & Gardens*, ph. Robin Matthews; R: *Woman & Home*, ph. Debi Treloar; p114-5 All ph. John Freeman; p116-7 All Robert Harding, TL: *Homes & Gardens*, ph. Stewart Grant; BL: *BBC Homes & Antiques*, ph. Brian Harrison; TR: *Homes & Gardens*; BR: *Country Homes & Interiors*, ph. Kim Sayer; p118-9 All Robert Harding, TL: *Homes & Gardens*, ph. John Mason; BL: *Homes & Ideas*, ph. Andrew Cameron; R: *Country Homes & Interiors*, ph. Tim Imrie; p120-1 All Robert Harding, All *Homes & Gardens*, TL: ph. Trevor Richards; BL: ph. Chris Drake; TR: ph. Tom Leighton; p122-3 All Robert Harding, All *Country Homes & Interiors*, TL: ph. Polly Wreford; BL: *Homes & Gardens*, ph. James Merrell; TR: ph. Mark Luscombe-Whyte; BR: ph. Bill Batten; p124-5 All Robert Harding, TL: *Homes & Gardens*, ph. Christopher Drake; BL: *Homes & Gardens*, ph. Jonathan Pilkington; TR: *Ideal Home*; BR: *Homes & Gardens*.